Contents

Introduction

Welcome to the extraordinary world of Bash scripting! Whether you're a seasoned Linux or Unix system administrator, a developer venturing into the command line, or a curious novice, this book will transform your interactions with your operating system.

The Versatile Power of Shell Scripting

Have you ever found yourself executing the same series of commands in your terminal again and again? Perhaps you're regularly backing up files, checking system resources, or processing data. Shell scripting empowers you to automate these tedious tasks, save precious time, and minimize the potential for errors.

Imagine an invisible assistant within your computer, effortlessly carrying out complex instructions at your command. That's the core of shell scripting. By crafting shell scripts, you'll have your computer working harder for you.

What is Bash?

The Bash shell is the default command-line interpreter on most Linux distributions, Unix-like systems, and macOS. It offers a robust programming environment built right into your operating system. Think of it as the bridge between you and the heart of your machine. With Bash scripting, you harness Bash's powerful abilities to control processes, interact with files, and manage your system seamlessly.

Why Learn Bash Scripting?

- **Automation Mastery:** Transform repetitive tasks into single, well-organized scripts. Imagine setting up daily backups with a few lines of code!
- **Increased Efficiency:** Stop wasting time with manual and error-prone processes. A well-written script can be a lifesaver.
- **Expanded Skillset:** Become a more versatile and valuable IT professional with scripting in your toolbox.
- **Powerful Customization:** Tailor your operating system environment to match your workflow perfectly.
- **The Joy of Creation:** There's something satisfying about solving problems with code, even at the command-line level. With practice, you'll write cleaner, more elegant scripts.

The Learning Journey

This book is your comprehensive guide to the art of Bash scripting. We'll start with the fundamental building blocks, such as variables, commands, and control structures. From there, we'll dive into more advanced concepts, including functions, wildcards, error handling, and debugging. Finally, we'll conquer specific applications such as text processing, automation, and system administration.

Prerequisites

This book assumes a basic comfort level with using the command line and a text editor. If you've never opened a terminal, it might be beneficial to explore some introductory resources on Linux fundamentals before diving into scripting.

Let's Get Started!

It's time to start wielding the power of the Bash shell and create scripts that streamline and optimize your work. Turn the page to join a world of efficient problem-solving and command-line creativity!

Additional Resources

- **The Linux Documentation Project (TLDP) Guide to Bash:** https://www.tldp.org/LDP/abs/html/
- **GNU Bash Manual:** https://www.gnu.org/software/bash/manual/bash.html
- **Linux Journey** (For beginners): https://linuxjourney.com/

Section 1:
Foundations of Shell Scripting

Introduction to Shell Scripting: Basics and Beyond

Welcome to the world of Bash scripting! In this chapter, we'll lay the foundation for your scripting journey, introducing core concepts and building essential skills. Understanding these early stages will streamline your progress throughout the book.

What is a Shell Script?

At its heart, a shell script is a simple text file containing a series of commands that your Linux, Unix, or macOS shell can execute. Picture it as a recipe the shell interpreter follows step-by-step to automate actions.

Why Script?

Here's the power of scripting:

- **Save Time:** A script does the heavy lifting by running a tedious command sequence with a single command.
- **Reduce Errors:** Once a script is working, it executes the same process perfectly each time, avoiding mistakes you might make if you were typing manually.
- **Consistency:** Whether you're running across one machine or many, scripts deliver consistency in setup and process.

- **Share and Expand:** You can share scripts with colleagues, and your scripts can be the building blocks for even larger and more complex programs.

Your First Bash Script

Let's create a simple "Hello World" script:

1. **Choose a Text Editor:** You can use basic editors like Nano or Vi/Vim, or more advanced IDEs. We'll stick to basics for now.
2. **Create the Script:**
   - Open your terminal and type `nano greetings.sh` to create a script called 'greetings.sh'.
   - Inside the file, paste the following lines:

```
#!/bin/bash
echo "Hello, Shell Scripting World!"
```

3. **Explanation:**
   - `#!/bin/bash`: This 'shebang' line declares which interpreter to use for executing this file. Here, it's the Bash shell.
   - `echo "Hello, Shell Scripting World!"`: This line is a simple command that will print the enclosed text to your terminal.
4. **Save and Exit:** In Nano, press Ctrl+X, then 'Y', then Enter to save.
5. **Make it Executable:** Type `chmod +x greetings.sh` to grant execute permissions to the script.
6. **Run the Script:** Type `./greetings.sh`. You should see the friendly greeting on your screen!

Essential Building Blocks

Let's dissect the key elements often found in a script:

- **Shebang:** Always declare the interpreter as seen above.
- **Comments:** Use # to add comments. This helps document your code and improves clarity.
- **Commands:** The heart of your script. This is where you use familiar Linux commands like `ls`, `grep`, `sed`, `awk`, etc.
- **Variables:** Like boxes in memory, these can store data such as a filename or the output of a command. We'll cover them in more detail soon.
- **Control Flow:** Conditional statements (e.g., `if`, `else`) and loops (e.g., `for`, `while`) tell the script what to do based on certain conditions or repeating tasks.

Beyond the Basics: Good Scripting Practices

- **Indentation:** Makes your code easily readable for you and others.
- **Meaningful names:** Name variables and functions descriptively.
- **Modularity:** Break scripts into smaller functions for reusability and easier maintenance.

Additional Resources

- **GNU Bash Manual:**
  https://www.gnu.org/software/bash/manual/bash.html
- **Linux Shell Scripting Tutorial (freeCodeCamp):**
  https://www.youtube.com/watch?v=v-F3YLd6oMw

Up Next

With the basics under your belt, we're ready to move into the intermediate territory! In the next chapter, we'll explore variables, command substitutions, arithmetic operations, and more. Get ready to script with style.

Advancing in Shell Scripting: Intermediate Concepts

With basic scripting under your belt, you're ready to expand your repertoire. This chapter explores concepts that turn rudimentary scripts into powerful tools, increasing your flexibility and the sophistication of your creations.

Variables: Storing and Handling Data

Variables are like labeled containers within your script that hold information. Let's explore how to work with them:

1. **Creating Variables:**
   ```
   my_variable="Hello"  # No spaces around the
   '=' sign
   ```
2. **Using Variables:**
   ```
   echo $my_variable   # Access the value using
   a '$' prefix
   ```
3. **Special Variables:**
   - $0: Holds the name of the script itself.
   - $1, $2, ... $9: Store command-line arguments passed to your script.
   - $@: Represents all arguments passed to the script.
   - $#: Stores the total number of arguments.
   - $$: Holds the Process ID (PID) of the currently running script.

Example: Handling Command-Line Arguments

```
#!/bin/bash

echo "This script is called: $0"

echo "You provided $# arguments"
```

```
echo "The first argument is: $1"
```

Arithmetic Operations

Bash can perform basic calculations. Here's how:

- **Using expr:** (Older method)
  ```
  result=$(expr 5 + 3)   # Store the result in
  a variable

  echo $result
  ```

- **Double Parentheses:** (Simpler)
  ```
  result=$(( 5 + 3 ))

  echo $result
  ```

Command Substitution: Capturing Command Output

This powerful technique lets you store the result of a command in a variable for further use. Syntax:

```
variable=$(command)    # Using backticks is an
older but valid alternative
```

Example: Finding Uptime

```
#!/bin/bash

uptime_output=$(uptime)

echo "The current system uptime is:
$uptime_output"
```

Conditional Statements: Making Script Decisions

Conditionals enable your scripts to execute different logic based on specified conditions:

- **The `if` Statement**

```
if [ condition ]; then

    # Commands to execute if the condition
is true

else

    # Commands to execute if the condition
is false

fi
```

- **Comparison Operators:**
    - `-eq`: Equal to
    - `-ne`: Not equal to
    - `-gt`: Greater than
    - `-lt`: Less than
    - `-ge`: Greater than or equal to
    - `-le`: Less than or equal to

File Test Operators: (e.g., to check if a file exists) * `-f`: File exists and is a regular file. * `-d`: File exists and is a directory.

Example: File Comparison

```
if [ file1 -nt file2 ]; then

    echo "file1 is newer than file2"

fi
```

Next Steps

Now that you understand variables, arithmetic, command substitution, and conditional logic, we're ready to tackle advanced techniques for professional-grade scripting in the next chapter.

Experiment with these concepts and solidify your command of them!

Additional Resources

- **Advanced Bash Scripting Guide (TLDP):**
  https://www.tldp.org/LDP/abs/html/
- **Conditional Expressions in Bash:**
  http://tldp.org/LDP/Bash-Beginners-Guide/html/sect_07_01.
  html

Shell Scripting Proficiency: Advanced Techniques

Having mastered intermediate concepts, your scripting toolkit is expanding at a phenomenal pace. This chapter explores refined techniques that separate experienced scripters from beginners. These strategies streamline efficiency and open new possibilities.

Arrays: Handling Structured Data

Arrays allow you to store multiple values as a single unit. Here's how to work with them in Bash:

1. **Creating an Array:**

```
my_array=("value1" "value2" "value3")
```

2. **Accessing Elements:**

```
echo ${my_array[0]}    # Access the first
element
echo ${my_array[1]}    # Access the second
element, etc.
```

3. **Iterating through an Array:**

```
for item in "${my_array[@]}"; do
    echo $item
done
```

Example: Processing Files in a Directory

```
files=(*.txt)    # Store all .txt files in the
current directory
for file in "${files[@]}"; do
```

```
    echo "Processing: $file"
    # Add commands to process each file
done
```

Regular Expressions (RegEx): Powerful Pattern Matching

Regular expressions define a search pattern you can use to
match, replace, or manipulate text. Bash and many other
command-line tools (like grep, sed, awk) utilize RegEx extensively.
**Note: A full tutorial on regular expressions is beyond the
scope of this chapter, but here's a taste:**

- **Basic Symbols**
    - . Matches any single character.
    - ^ Matches the beginning of a line.
    - $ Matches the end of a line.
    - * Matches zero or more occurrences of the
      preceding character.

- **Example: Finding emails**

```
grep -E
"\b[A-Za-z0-9._%+-]+@[A-Za-z0-9.-]+\.[A-Za-z
]{2,}\b" input_file.txt
```

Input/Output Redirection

Redirection lets you manage data flow into and out of your scripts:

- **> Output Redirection:** Sends standard output of a
  command to a file, overwriting any existing content.

```
ls -l > directory_listing.txt
```

- **>> Output Appending:** Adds script output to the end of a file.

```
echo "New error message" >> errors.log
```

- **< Input Redirection:** Feeds the contents of a file as input to a command.

```
sort < names.txt
```

Pipelines (|): Chaining Commands

Pipelines connect the output of one command to the input of another. It's data transformation magic:

```
ls -l | grep "Aug" | awk '{print $9}'  # List
files, filter for August, print filenames
```

Process Substitution: Temporary Data Streams

This advanced technique creates temporary named pipes or files you can manipulate within your script. Syntax:

```
diff <(command1) <(command2)
```

Example: Comparing Sorted Outputs

```
diff <(ls -l | sort) <(ls -al | sort)
```

Remember Practice is essential! Combine these techniques to solve scripting challenges that seem impossible at first glance.

Additional Resources

- **Regular-Expressions.info**
  https://www.regular-expressions.info/
- **IO Redirection in Bash**
  https://www.tldp.org/LDP/abs/html/io-redirection.html

In the Next Chapter

Let's move to the fourth and final chapter in the "Foundations" section – Expert Shell Scripting. Get ready to learn innovation and scripting mastery strategies!

Expert Shell Scripting: Mastery and Innovations

You have all the essential tools of scripting! Now, take steps towards true expertise. An expert scripter possesses the following qualities, which we'll focus on this chapter:

Efficiency and Elegance

- **Performance Optimization:** Profile your scripts to find bottlenecks (the `time` command is helpful). Are heavy loops slowing you down? Explore faster algorithms or tools.
- **Concise Code:** Look for ways to combine operations – Can you do with fewer variables? Does piping eliminate temporary files? Remember, readability also matters!
- **Know Your Tools:** Deep knowledge of bash built-ins and powerful command-line utilities enables crafting concise, resource-efficient scripts.

Robust and Error-proof

- **Defensive Programming:** Assume everything can go wrong! Input validation, checking the success of each command (often by `if [ $? -eq 0 ]; then ...`), and careful error handling make your scripts reliable under unexpected conditions.
- **Test Cases:** Design a few key test cases to simulate your script's functionality, even before it's fully written. It helps to build scripts correctly from the start, and makes them fail predictably.
- **Meaningful Error Messages:** When things do go wrong, provide informative context so both you and your users can easily identify and rectify issues.

Flexibility and Adaptability

- **Modularity:** Create script libraries of well-defined, reusable functions (we'll cover some tips soon). These become versatile Lego blocks in new programs.
- **Parameterization:** Make scripts user-friendly by accepting variable input via command-line arguments or configuration files.
- **Alternative Solutions:** For every scripting challenge, there are likely multiple approaches. Explore to increase your repertoire, and tailor solutions to problems intelligently.

Advanced Scripting Techniques

- **Subshells:** Create subshells (a new copy of Bash within your script) to isolate variables and change directories without disrupting the main script's execution environment. Syntax: (`commands`)
- **Traps:** These let your script respond to signals and interrupts during execution. This is great for custom cleanup/recovery when a user hits Ctrl+C. See the `trap` command for details.

Best Practices and Refinements

- **Descriptive Naming Conventions:** Consistent names for variables, functions, and files aid in comprehension and maintaining your scripts months or years later.
- **Code Formatting:** Proper indentation and spacing (your text editor will help) separate script segments for easy visual parsing.
- **Documentation:** Leave clear comments to explain intricate sections of code, even to yourself! External documentation files (READMEs) are best for long scripts and projects.

Additional Resources

- **ShellCheck – Find Bugs in Your Shell Scripts:**
  https://www.shellcheck.net/
- **ExplainShell – Get Explanations for Shell Commands:**
  https://explainshell.com/

Continuous Learning

The realm of Bash scripting is expansive. Staying curious, seeking creative solutions, and learning from resources and expert communities will lead you to scripting mastery.

- Explore community-created packages and tools that extend your functionality and save time.
- Contribute to online documentation (like wikis) or projects yourself, learning by teaching!

Concluding the Foundation

With practice, these strategies will become second nature. Soon, creating polished Bash scripts will be an instinct. You're ready for more specialized exploration: return codes, advanced functions, wildcards, etc.!

Section 2:
Understanding Return Codes and Exit Statuses

The Essentials of Exit Statuses and Return Codes

Imagine your Bash scripts as individual messengers sent on various errands. Exit statuses and return codes are the secret messages these processes hand back, relaying vital information about their missions' success or failure. Mastering this hidden language is crucial for robust and intelligent script construction.

What are Exit Statuses?

- Every command and script running on your Linux, Unix, or macOS system terminates with an exit status.
- It's a numeric code, typically between 0 and 255, signaling the outcome.
- Conventionally, a *zero* (0) exit status indicates success, while non-zero values usually represent different types of errors or unexpected results.

Accessing Exit Statuses in Bash

Bash stores the last executed command's exit status in a special variable named $?. Here's how to check it:

1. **Run a command:**

```
ls -l
```

2. **Check the exit status:**

```
echo $?
```

A '0' should appear since `ls -l` will typically execute successfully.

Example: Handling a Missing File

```
ls -l missing_file.txt
echo $?   # This will likely be non-zero
```

Return Codes in Scripts

- **The exit Command:** Within your scripts, the `exit` command lets you explicitly specify the exit status for the whole script.
- **Implicit Exit:** If you don't use `exit`, your script inherits the exit status of the last command it executed.

Example: Customized Exit Status

```bash
#!/bin/bash

some_command  # Imagine this command can
sometimes fail

if [ $? -ne 0 ]; then  # Checking the exit status
of 'some_command'
    echo "Something went wrong!"
    exit 1  # Custom error code
else
    echo "Success!"
    exit 0
```

```
fi
```

Common Exit Status Meanings

While exit codes above 128 signal a process terminated by a 'signal,' those below 128 are command-specific. However, some broad conventions exist:

- **0:** Success
- **1:** General, unspecified error
- **2:** Misuse of Shell built-in commands

Beyond the Basics

- Commands often provide more refined error codes (see their documentation). Understanding these helps craft specific troubleshooting logic within your scripts.
- It's often best to have your scripts exit with custom, easily identifiable exit statuses for easier error management.

Why Do Exit Statuses Matter?

1. **Flow Control:** Use `if` statements with $? for conditional logic. One part of your script executes on success, another on failure.
2. **Error Handling:** Gracefully addressing expected error cases improves the resilience of your scripts.
3. **Automation and Chaining Scripts:** Scripts within automated chains or cron jobs often communicate primarily through exit statuses. Ensuring consistency is key.

Additional Resources

- **Exit Codes with Special Meanings (TLDP):** https://www.tldp.org/LDP/abs/html/exitcodes.html
- **Advanced Bash Scripting Guide: Exit Codes:** https://www.tldp.org/LDP/abs/html/exit-status.html

Advanced Interpretations of Return Codes in Scripting

In the previous chapter, you mastered the fundamentals of exit statuses. Now, let's explore how to utilize the specific exit codes returned by commands to create truly intelligent and adaptable scripts.

Beyond Success or Failure

Many commands provide granular exit codes that reveal the exact reason for a failure. Deciphering these codes takes your error handling to new levels. Let's illustrate this with a few examples:

- **grep (Exit Codes)**
  - 0: Match found.
  - 1: No match found.
  - 2: Error (bad regex, file issues, etc.)

Example: Specific grep Error Handling

```
grep "search_pattern" file.txt


if [ $? -eq 0 ]; then

    echo "Pattern found!"

elif [ $? -eq 1 ]; then

    echo "Pattern not found."

else

    echo "An error occurred during the search."
```

```
fi
```

- **diff (Exit Codes)**
    - ○ 0: Files are identical.
    - ○ 1: Files are different.
    - ○ 2: Error (inaccessible files, etc.)

Example: File Changes

```
diff file1.txt file2.txt
```

```
if [ $? -eq 0 ]; then

    echo "Files have not changed."

elif [ $? -eq 1 ]; then

    echo "Files are different. Update needed."

else

    echo "Error comparing files."

fi
```

Customizing Your Scripts

Incorporating advanced error interpretation gives finer control over your scripts:

- **Specific Error Messages:** Instead of generic "failed" messages, provide context based on the exact issue.
- **Automated Remediation:** Can your script fix some errors directly? Perhaps file not found could trigger a download to try again.
- **Informed Logging:** Detailed logs aid in troubleshooting, even when you might not personally experience the failure.

Strategies for Discovering Exit Codes

Here's how to find the return code meanings for the commands you frequently use:

1. **Manual Pages (man)** Search man pages (e.g., `man grep`, `man diff`) for sections titled "Exit Status" or "Diagnostics."
2. **Command Documentation:** Often, online wikis or command-specific documentation websites list and explain exit codes.
3. **Experimentation:** Purposely induce errors (bad file names, etc.) and examine the exit status using `echo $?`

Caution with Assumptions

- Not all commands provide detailed exit codes. It's essential to consult reliable documentation sources to avoid surprises.
- Exit code meanings can sometimes slightly differ between implementations of the same command (e.g., GNU vs BSD-like systems). Test on your target systems.

Best Practices

- **Start Broad:** Check if a process succeeded or failed (0 vs. non-zero), then move toward more specific interpretation if it helps your case.
- **Log Exit Codes:** Even if your script doesn't immediately take advanced action, include error codes in logs for later analysis.

Additional Resources

- **GNU Coreutils Manuals:** (Commands common in most Linux distros)
  https://www.gnu.org/software/coreutils/manual/

- **Linux Documentation Project (TLDP):**
  https://www.tldp.org/

Up Next

You now understand how to decode exit statuses for sophisticated decision-making within your scripts. In the next chapter, let's demonstrate practical real-world applications of exit status handling.

Practical Demonstrations of Exit Status Utilization

Theory is essential, but nothing solidifies concepts like seeing them in action. Let's explore common scripting tasks and how integrating exit status interpretation takes them to the next level.

Scenario 1: Robust File Backups

```
#!/bin/bash

backup_file="/path/to/important_data.txt"
backup_destination="/backup/location"

cp $backup_file $backup_destination   # Attempt
backup

if [ $? -eq 0 ]; then
    echo "Backup successful!"
else
    echo "Backup failed. Check permissions or
disk space."
    # Optionally add logic to send an email or
alert
fi
```

- **Enhancements:** This goes far beyond "did it work?". Error checking could inform if space is tight, permissions wrong, etc. This script is a better citizen!

Scenario 2: Dependency Checks

```
#!/bin/bash
```

```
command -v unzip >/dev/null 2>&1  # Check if
'unzip' is installed

if [ $? -ne 0 ]; then
    echo "'unzip' is required. Please install."
    exit 1
fi

# ... Code that relies on unzip can safely
proceed here
```

- **Importance:** Prevents obscure crashes mid-script due to missing tools. User-friendly messages guide your audience to fix the problem early.

Scenario 3: Network Troubleshooting

```
#!/bin/bash

ping -c 2 www.google.com

if [ $? -ne 0 ]; then
    echo "Internet connection appears offline.
Check your network."
else
    echo "Connected to the internet."
fi
```

- **Diagnostic Tool:** Not just error handling, but active confirmation. A small script like this could be incorporated into system startup!

Scenario 4: Cascading Logic

```bash
#!/bin/bash

download_data "http://data_source/latest.csv"

if [ $? -ne 0 ]; then
    echo "Data download failed. Aborting
execution"
    exit 2
fi

process_data "latest.csv"

if [ $? -ne 0 ]; then
    echo "Processing failed. Check data format or
processing script."
fi

# ... Further steps relying on processing success
```

- **Interdependent Steps:** Smart checks at each stage control script flow. Unique script exit codes help isolate failure points in troubleshooting.

Scenario 5: Customized Retry Logic

```bash
#!/bin/bash

attempts=0
max_attempts=3

while [ $attempts -lt $max_attempts ]; do
    rsync -avz remote_folder/ ./local_backup/
    if [ $? -eq 0 ]; then
```

```
        echo "Backup successful after $attempts
tries"
        break  # Exit loop on success
    fi
    let attempts=attempts+1
    echo "Backup failed. Retrying in 5
seconds..."
    sleep 5
done
```

- **Persistence over Flaky Conditions:** Network hiccups happen! Retries plus spacing make this more likely to eventually succeed.

Beyond Simple Scripts

Exit status mastery shines in these areas:

- **Cron Jobs:** Clear email communication on tasks, successes, AND failures is important for automated management.
- **Script Libraries:** Functions you write return success or failure signals (using `exit [code]`) that become usable building blocks later.
- **Complex Pipelines:** Where a long process chain exists, check returns between steps to catch trouble early, not deep in execution.

Additional Resources

- **Linux Journal – Guide to Using Exit Codes:** https://www.linuxjournal.com/content/return-values-bash-functions

Let's Keep Building

As your scripting toolkit grows, so does the need for effective error management. Understanding exit statuses and making your scripts adapt is a hallmark of professional Bash programming.

Section 3:
The Art of Shell Functions

Crafting Basic Functions in Shell

Functions are a powerful tool that elevate your Bash scripts from sequences of commands to well-organized, reusable modular programs. Imagine them as miniature scripts within your larger script!

Why Use Functions?

- **Code Readability:** They break down complex scripts into understandable blocks, each carrying out a specific task.
- **Reusability:** Write a function once, and call it as many times as needed within the same script, or even across multiple scripts.
- **Modularity:** Enhances maintainability. Changes isolated to a function are less likely to break other parts of the script.
- **Testability:** You can test small functions independently, improving code reliability.

Basic Function Syntax

Here's the simplest format for creating a function in Bash:

```
function_name() {
    commands
}
```

Example: Greeting Function

```
function say_hello() {
    echo "Hello there!"
}
```

Calling Your Function

Simply type the function's name to execute it, like a regular command:

```
say_hello  #  This will print "Hello there!"
```

Passing Arguments to Functions

Functions become even more flexible when they can accept input:

1. **Positional Arguments:** Inside the function, reference them as $1 (first argument), $2 (second argument), and so on.
2. **Example: Personalized Greeting**

```
function greet_user() {
    echo "Hello, $1!"
}
```

```
greet_user "Alice"  # This will output "Hello,
Alice!"
```

Returning Values from Functions

While you can use echo within a function for output, more often, you'll want to use returned values. Let's explore:

- **The return Statement:** Used to send a numeric value (exit status) back to the main script.

- **Accessing Return Values:** Like exit statuses, access with $? after calling the function.

Example: File Check Function

```
function check_file() {
    if [ -f "$1" ]; then
        return 0  # Success
    else
        return 1  # Error
    fi
}


check_file "/path/to/file.txt"

if [ $? -eq 0 ]; then
    echo "File exists."
else
    echo "File not found."
fi
```

Using Functions Effectively

1. **Function Names:** Choose descriptive names that indicate their purpose (backup_files, calculate_average).
2. **Keep Them Focused:** Each function should have a clear and single responsibility.
3. **Indentation Matters:** Always indent code within functions for readability.

Local Variables

By default, variables inside a function are global, meaning they impact the entire script. To confine variables to the function's scope, declare them local:

```
function some_task() {
```

```
    local temporary_file="/tmp/temp.txt"
    # Work with the temporary_file
}
```

Additional Resources

- **Advanced Bash Scripting: Functions:**
  https://www.tldp.org/LDP/abs/html/functions.html
- **GreyCat's Wiki: Bash Functions:**
  http://mywiki.wooledge.org/BashGuide/Functions

Mastering Basics Sets the Stage

As you progress in crafting functions, you'll discover techniques for passing more complex data, advanced flow control within functions, and how they enable the creation of sophisticated Bash programs.

Next Up: Chapter 9 will help you enhance your script's capability with intermediate function concepts.

Enhancing Scripts with Intermediate Functions

With strong basics, you're ready to refine your function toolkit. Mastering these concepts will add sophistication, flexibility, and power to your Bash programming.

Passing Multiple Arguments

Often, your functions need more than one piece of input. Here's how to provide multiple arguments:

```
function process_data() {
    filename="$1"
    output_directory="$2"
    # ...process the data from $filename and
store it in $output_directory
}

process_data "input.csv" "/results"
```

- Remember: Inside the function, arguments are referenced as $1, $2, $3, and so on.

Returning Text Values

While usually, functions communicate using a numerical return code (`return [number]`), they can also send back text:

```
function get_system_info() {
    os_name=$(uname -s)
    kernel_version=$(uname -r)
    output="Operating System: $os_name
    Kernel: $kernel_version"
    echo "$output"  # Return the text output
```

```
}

info=$(get_system_info)   # Capture the entire
output in a variable
echo "$info"
```

Arrays as Function Arguments

Let's pass an entire array into a function:

```
function print_items() {
    local items_array=("$@")   # Access all passed
arguments as an array

    for item in "${items_array[@]}"; do
        echo $item
    done
}

my_items=("apple" "banana" "orange")
print_items "${my_items[@]}"
```

Note: It's essential to pass arrays with `"${array_name[@]}"` syntax (including quotes and [@]) to preserve any elements containing spaces.

Sourcing Function Libraries

For maintainability, break up scripts into files containing shared functions. Use `.` (dot) or `source` command:

```
#  In file 'my_functions.sh'
function calculate_average() {
    # Function code...
}

#  In your main script
```

```
. my_functions.sh   # Or 'source my_functions.sh'
calculate_average  #  Now you can call this
function!
```

Input Validation Inside Functions

Functions are the perfect place to sanitize and validate their input:

```
function create_backup() {
    if [ -z "$1" ]; then  #  Missing filename?
        echo "Error: please provide a filename."
        return 1
    fi

    # ...rest of your backup creation logic
}
```

Tips for Intermediate Function Design

- **Document with Comments:** Clarify a function's purpose and parameters, especially as they become complex.
- **Test Thoroughly:** Have test cases for each of your functions.
- **Consider Global vs. Local Variables:** Be mindful of the scope to avoid unexpected clashes in complex scripts.

Additional Resources

- **How to Pass Arrays to Bash Functions:** http://tldp.org/LDP/Bash-Beginners-Guide/html/sect_25_05.html
- **Advanced Bash Scripting: I/O Redirection within Functions:** https://www.tldp.org/LDP/abs/html/io-redirection.html

Mastering Advanced Functional Techniques in Shell

You've harnessed the power of functions, but they hold greater depths. Unlocking these advanced tactics makes you a true power user.

Nested Functions

Functions can define other functions *within* themselves. Nested functions are like hidden toolsets! These are mainly used for helper functions.

```
function outer_function() {

    function helper_function() {

        # Code only available within
'outer_function'

    }



    helper_function  # Can be called within
'outer_function'

}



# helper_function CANNOT be called from the main
script
```

- **Benefits:** Encapsulation of specialized logic, keeping function code focused, avoiding global namespace pollution.

Recursion: Functions Calling Themselves

A recursive function elegantly solves problems broken into smaller, self-similar pieces (like searching through directories). Exercise caution – recursion can consume significant resources if not done carefully.

Example: Factorial Calculation

```
function factorial() {

    if [ $1 -le 1 ]; then

        echo 1

    else

        local prev_factorial=$(factorial $(( $1 - 1 )))

        echo $(( $1 * prev_factorial))

    fi

}



factorial 5  # Calculates 5! (= 120)
```

Indirect Variable References

Access variables *whose names are stored in other variables*:

```
function work_with_data() {

    local data_var_name="$1"

    local value="${!data_var_name}"   # Use
'!var_name' for indirection



    echo "The value is: $value"

}



my_data=42

data_var_name="my_data"

work_with_data "$data_var_name" # Outputs "The
value is: 42"
```

- **Use Cases:** Dynamically working with similarly named variables (data_1, data_2, etc.), or if variable names themselves come from user input.

Advanced Debugging within Functions

- **set -x (Debug Tracing):** Inside a function, temporarily use set -x to print each line of its execution for troubleshooting. Use set +x to turn it off.
- **trap for Custom Cleanup:** Handle signals (Ctrl+C) or errors for temporary files, etc.
https://www.tldp.org/LDP/Bash-Beginners-Guide/html/sect_12_02.html

Scope Quirks to Conquer

- **Variables Declared Outside Without `local` Are Global:** Be mindful. Unexpected modifications cause bugs.
- **`return` Can Only Send Numbers:** Using stdout within functions for text values is more flexible.
- **Use Care with Recursion:** Easy to create unintentional infinite loops or exhaust memory in very deep recursions.

Best Practices

- **Strategic Indirection:** Indirect referencing is powerful, but sparingly used keeps code clearer.
- **Recursion Use-cases:** Factorials are simple; tree-like data structures (file systems) are much more common use cases.

Additional Resources

- **Recursive Functions in Bash:** http://tldp.org/LDP/Bash-Beginners-Guide/html/sect_09_07.html)
- **Advanced Bash Scripting: Variable Indirection:** http://tldp.org/LDP/Bash-Beginners-Guide/html/sect_10_03.html

Beyond Functional Limits

While functions bring modularity, for tasks needing data structures (think lists, tables), more structured scripting languages often suit better. Bash excels at command gluing!

Next Steps

Up next, we'll dive into 'wildcards', giving you surgical control over files and paths in your scripts! Let me know when you're ready.

Section 4:

The Power of Wildcards in Scripting

Wildcard Basics: Enhancing Script Flexibility

Wildcards are special characters that expand into flexible filename patterns, giving Bash scripts incredible adaptability. Forget listing hundreds of files; a few well-placed wildcards do the trick!

The Essentials

- **The Asterisk (*)** This is your workhorse. It matches *zero or more* characters.
    - `report_*.txt` Matches "report_1.txt", "report_final.txt", "report_old.txt", etc.
- **The Question Mark (?)** Matches *exactly one* character.
    - `data??.csv` Matches "data01.csv", "data99.csv", but NOT "data100.csv" or "data.csv"

Basic Use Cases

Let's see some in action:

- **Listing Files Selectively:**

```
ls *.pdf  # Lists all PDF files in the
current directory
```

- **Copying with Patterns:**

```
cp project_*.old /backup/  # Copy old
project files to a backup folder
```

- **Deleting by Wildcards (Use CAUTION!)**

```
rm temp_*    # Deletes files starting with
"temp_"
```

Combining Wildcards

The real power comes from combining these for specific matchings:

```
mv my_data_??-2023.log /old_logs/
 # Moves logs like 'my_data_01-2023.log',
'my_data_15-2023.log', etc.
```

Beyond the Basics: Brackets

- **Character Sets ([ ])** Match *any single character* inside the brackets.
  - `file[123].txt` Matches "file1.txt", "file2.txt", "file3.txt"
- **Ranges ([a-z])** Match any character within the range.
  - `backup_[A-Z]*.zip` Matches backup files with a starting capital letter.

Important Precautions

- **Unexpected Expansion:** If no files match the pattern, the wildcard often remains as is. Example: `rm *.zip` may not delete anything… if no .zip files exist!

- **Quoting Matters:** In some cases, you want to prevent expansion. Single or double quotes (' or ") prevent the shell from interpreting the wildcard.

Practical Examples

1. **Image Conversion**

```
for file in *.jpg; do
    convert "$file" "${file%.jpg}.png"
    # Replaces '.jpg' extension with '.png'
done
```

2. **Processing Recent Logs**

```
tail -f log_$(date +%Y-%m-%d).log
 #  Tails today's log file (based on the
date)
```

Additional Resources

- **Explainshell.com** https://explainshell.com/ (Interactive Wildcard Demonstration)
- **Filenames and Pathnames in Shell:** https://www.gnu.org/software/bash/manual/html_node/Filename-Expansion.html (Detailed information)

Up Next

Now that you understand the core wildcards, we'll dive deeper into combining them and other techniques to craft sophisticated and flexible script patterns.

Intermediate Wildcard Usage in Scripts

You've grasped the wildcard fundamentals. Now, let's explore how they empower your scripts to adapt and work smarter, not harder.

Negation with !

Often, you want to *exclude* files matching a pattern:

```
rm !(*.zip)  # Delete everything EXCEPT .zip
files
```

```
# Find non-hidden files (those NOT starting with
'.')

find . -type f ! -name ".*"
```

Fine-Tuning Selections

- **Limiting to Files or Directories**
  - `ls -d */` Lists only directories (by including a trailing '/')
  - `ls -p | grep -v /` Lists only regular files
- **Matching the Beginning of a File**
  - `^report*.csv` Finds files specifically starting with 'report'

Brace Expansion: Creating Variations

Not strictly a wildcard, but similar! Use { } for generating several filenames. Not as flexible as wildcards, but neat:

```
mkdir project_{a,b,c}  # Creates directories
project_a, project_b, project_c

touch report_{01..05}.txt  # Creates
report_01.txt through report_05.txt
```

Selective Backups

```
today=$(date +%Y-%m-%d)

backup_name="system_backup_$today.tar.gz"

tar -czvf $backup_name /etc /home  # Exclude
logs, cache, etc.

        --exclude=/var/log --exclude=/var/cache
```

Case-Insensitive matching

By default, wildcard matches are case-sensitive. To get around this (use carefully!)

- **shopt Command:**
  ```
  shopt -s nocasematch  # Turns on
  case-insensitive matching

  shopt -u nocasematch  # Turns off
  case-insensitive matching
  ```

Matching across Directories (Caution!)

- **Globstar (**) (Bash 4.0+)** Enables recursive wildcard matching through subdirectories. **Use carefully due to performance impact on large directories.**

```
rm -rf **/temp_*  # Delete all files/folders
starting with "temp_" recursively
```

When It's NOT Quite Wildcards

Some complex matching is difficult with pure wildcards. Remember 'power tools' exist:

- **The `find` Command:** More refined filtering by file size, modification times, etc.
  ```
  find . -name "*.tmp" -mtime +7 -exec rm {} \;  #Find and delete old .tmp files
  ```
- **Regular Expressions (`grep`, `sed`, etc.):** These provide a deeper level of pattern matching precision.

Additional Resources

- **The Linux Documentation Project: Pattern Matching**
  http://tldp.org/LDP/abs/html/patterns.html
- **Brace Expansion in Bash**
  https://www.gnu.org/software/bash/manual/html_node/Brace-Expansion.html

Best Practices

- **Test Wildcards:** Double-check what matches your pattern before 'rm' or destructive commands. echo is your friend – it echoes filenames without action.
- **Clarity Before Conciseness:** While complex wildcards are possible, favor readability of your code if others (or future you!) need to understand it.

Coming Up

Next, we'll see how to combine wildcards with loops and commands to unlock a new level of scripting efficiency in "Integrating Wildcards into Advanced Scripts".

Integrating Wildcards into Advanced Scripts

The true power of wildcards shines when paired with commands, loops, and the vast toolbox Bash offers. They give you a way to select precisely the 'inputs' to your script operations.

File Operations in Bulk

```bash
# Renaming with Pattern Matching

for file in project_data_*.csv; do

    mv "$file" "${file/project_data/final_data}"

    # Replaces 'project_data' with 'final_data'
in filenames

done



# Archive a Specific Date Range

mkdir daily_backups

tar -czf "daily_backups/backup_$(date
+%Y-%m-%d).tar.gz" log_2023-11-??.txt
```

Targeted System Maintenance

```bash
# Disk Space Cleanup (Find large files, preview
before deleting!)
```

```
find /var/log -type f -size +50M -exec ls -lh {}
\;
```

```
# Rotate system logs, but keep some history

gzip -9 < /var/log/syslog >
/var/log/syslog.old.gz  # Compress old logfile

echo "" > /var/log/syslog  # Clear current log
(messages keep logging here)
```

Looping for Advanced Selections

```
# Check integrity of backup files

for backup in *.zip; do

    if ! zip -T "$backup"; then  # Check zip
integrity with '-T'

        echo "WARNING: Corrupted backup found:
$backup"

    fi

 done
```

```
# Match by Date with 'find' (careful - modify
action as needed!)

find . -maxdepth 1 -name "temp_*" -mtime +14
-exec rm {} \;
```

```
#  Delete 'temp_*' older than 14 days
```

Pitfalls and Precautions

- **"Too Many Files" Errors:** When wildcards expand to massive file sets, they can overload commands. Pre-test, or break into smaller batches within your script.
- **Hidden Files (. *):** Remember, a normal * doesn't match these unless your purpose is to include those too!
- **Cross-Filesystem Issues:** The recursive ** (globstar) sometimes has trouble when file targets span different mounted filesystems.

Beyond the Script: Command Line Comfort

The same wildcard skills enhance day-to-day usage:

- **Quick Counts:** echo *.pdf | wc -w (Count PDF files)
- **Filtering ls:** ls -l | grep ".txt$" (See only '.txt' files)
- **Cleanup:** rm -i core.* (Interactive delete any core dump files)

When Even Wildcards Aren't Enough

There are limits! For really intricate filtering, you might need:

- **Subshells:** mv $(find . -name "*.tmp") trash/ (Pipe result of 'find' to 'mv')
- **External Data:** For tasks like "modify files matching this list on a website", scripting shines at getting the data, but text processing tools excel at filtering that.

Additional Resources

- **GNU Parallel (for batch processing with wildcards):** https://www.gnu.org/software/parallel/
- **When are wildcards expanded?** http://tldp.org/LDP/Bash-Beginners-Guide/html/sect_03_04.html

The Next Level

We're about to conclude our deep dive into wildcards with "Practical Applications: Wildcard Scripting Scenarios". Let's see real-world use examples!

Practical Applications: Wildcard Scripting Scenarios

Wildcards aren't just theoretical. Let's bring them to life with common tasks scripters frequently face. Adapt and extend these as the building blocks for your own solutions!

Scenario 1: Image Processing

Task: Convert PNG images to optimized JPGs, create thumbnails, and add a watermark.

```
for image in *.png; do

    convert "$image" -quality 80
"${image%.png}.jpg"

    convert "$image" -resize 200x200
"thumbnail_${image%.png}.jpg"

    composite -gravity center watermark.png
"${image%.png}.jpg"
"watermarked_${image%.png}.jpg"

done
```

Breakdown:

- ***.png: ** Selects all PNG files for processing.
- **${image%.png}.jpg:** Clever filename manipulation removes '.png' for clean JPEG naming.
- **ImageMagick's convert:** A powerful command-line image tool does the conversions, resizing, and compositing.

Scenario 2: Website Backup (Selective)

Task: Download certain directories of a website, excluding cache and dynamically generated content.

```
wget -r -np -nH --cut-dirs=2 -R ".tmp*,*cache*"
http://www.example.com/wp-content/
http://www.example.com/assets/
```

Breakdown:

- **wget:** Robust file downloading utility. Options used here (-r recursive, -np no parent directories, etc.) are vital! See full manual.
- **-R ".tmp*,*cache*":** Powerful exclusion pattern preventing unwanted clutter.

Scenario 3: Log Rotation and Compression

Task: Compress logs older than a week, retain two months worth, delete the rest.

```
find /var/log -name "*.log" -mtime +7 -exec gzip
{} \;

find /var/log -name "*.gz" -mtime +60 -delete
```

Breakdown:

- **find as our Filtering Master:** Here, finding files based on modification time.
- **Caution Note:** Ensure /var/log is the correct path on your system. Test deletions carefully!

Scenario 4: System Cleanup Script

Task: Find and prompt for deletion of potentially large, space-hogging files.

```
search_dirs=("/home" "/var/cache" "/tmp")  # Add
directories as needed

for dir in "${search_dirs[@]}"; do

    find "$dir" -type f -size +100M -printf "%p -
%s bytes\n" -exec bash -c 'read -p "Delete this
file? [y/N]: $1" answer; [[ $answer = [yY] ]] &&
rm "$1"' _ {} \;

done
```

Breakdown:

- **Arrays for Organization:** Keeping search folders tidy.
- **Interactive Safety:** Uses read -p for per-file deletion confirmation.

Keep The Momentum

- Each system, user, and task brings unique needs. Use these as starting points and expand!
- Explore command-line tools specific to your field (data processing, networking, etc.) – many can be woven into scripts using wildcards.

Additional Resources

- **Linux Journal: File Globbing**
  https://www.linuxjournal.com/content/globbing-and-pattern-matching-bash
- **Awesome Shell: A curated list of resources**
  https://github.com/alebcay/awesome-shell

Next: Decision-Making Power

Wildcards provide flexible input to actions. Upcoming, we'll explore 'case statements', giving your scripts the ability to execute the *right* actions based on conditions.

Section 5:
Decision Making with Case Statements and Logic Constructs

Basics of Case Statements in Scripting

So far, your scripts have followed a mostly linear path. Imagine them as simple robots. The case statement teaches your scripts to think, making choices to better interact with users and environments.

The Concept: Choices Based on Patterns

Here's the essential structure of a case statement:

```
case $variable in
    pattern1)
        commands_if_pattern1_matches
        ;;  #Indicates end of pattern1 section
    pattern2)
        commands_if_pattern2_matches
        ;;
    *)  # Default 'catch-all' if nothing else
matches
        commands_for_no_match
        ;;
 esac  #  'case' spelled backwards
```

How it Works

1. The value of $variable is compared to each of the patterns sequentially.
2. If a match is found, the corresponding commands execute.
3. The double semicolon ; ; is essential to mark the end of each pattern section.

Example: Basic File Type Handling

```
file_to_process="report.pdf"
case "$file_to_process" in
    *.txt)
        echo "Processing a text file..."
        ;;
    *.pdf)
        echo "Converting PDF to text..."
        pdftotext "$file_to_process"
        ;;
    *.zip)
        echo "Extracting archive..."
        unzip "$file_to_process"
        ;;
    *)
        echo "Unknown file type!"
        ;;
esac
```

Key Points for Patterns

- Patterns use wildcard-like matching:
  - ? matches a single character
  - * matches zero or more characters
- Be mindful of pattern order – the first match wins!

Common Applications

- **User Menus:** Present a list of options, take action based on choice.
- **Command-Line Argument Handling:** Different behavior based on options (e.g., -v for verbose output).
- **File Type Handling:** (Like the example above)
- **System State Evaluation:** Checking if services are running, etc.

Best Practices

- **Default Case:** Include the *) 'catch-all' to handle unexpected input.
- **Indentation:** Keep code within each pattern block readable.
- **Combine with Input:** Often, input via command-line arguments works great:

```
case "$1" in  # Using 1st argument to the script
    start)
        #Commands to start a process
        ;;
    #... more patterns here ...
esac
```

Additional Resources

- **GNU Bash Manual: Case Statements**
  https://www.gnu.org/software/bash/manual/html_node/Conditional-Constructs.html
- **ExplainShell with a case Example**
  https://explainshell.com/

Power Up Your Scripts

The case statement makes your scripts reactive to environment and user choices. Next, in "Advanced Case Logic in Shell Scripts", we'll explore extending it for even more sophisticated behaviors.

Advanced Case Logic in Shell Scripts

You understand the case statement fundamentals. Now, unlock its hidden flexibility to make your scripts even more responsive and capable.

Multiple Matches per Pattern

Using the 'or' operator (|) lets you combine patterns under a single case branch:

```
case "$response" in
    yes | y | YES | Yes)
        echo "Affirmative!"
        ;;
    n | no | NO)
        echo "Negative!"
        ;;
    *)
        echo "Please enter yes or no."
        ;;
esac
```

Capturing Parts of Patterns

Use parenthesis ( ) to capture portions of a pattern, assigning them to variables:

```
case "$filename" in

    backup_([0-9]{4}-[0-9]{2}-[0-9]{2}).tar.gz)

        backup_date="${BASH_REMATCH[1]}"   #
YYYY-MM-DD part

        echo "Backup from: $backup_date"

        ;;

    *)

        echo "Not a valid backup filename
format."

        ;;

esac
```

- **Note:** Parentheses enable a regex-like feature; ${BASH_REMATCH} array holds captured values.

Nested Case Statements

Decision trees! Place another case within a pattern's code for a second layer of decision-making:

```
case "$1" in

    start)

        case "$2" in
```

```
        production)

            run_production_server

            ;;

        test)

            run_test_server

            ;;

        *)

            echo "Specify environment
('production' or 'test')"

            ;;

        esac

        ;;

    #  More primary options....

esac
```

Example: Enhanced File Processor

```
case "$file" in

    *.csv)

        echo "CSV detected. Do you want to:"

        select action in "Calculate Stats"
"Filter Data" "Exit" ; do
```

```
        case "$action" in

            "Calculate Stats")

                # Code here...

                ;;

            "Filter Data")

                # Code here...

                ;;

                # ...

            esac

            break  # Break from inner 'select'
loop

        done

        ;;

    # ... Additional file types ...

esac
```

Practical Tips

- **Testing Nested case** : Work from the inside out for correct branching logic.
- **Functions Enhance Readability:** Move code in large pattern blocks into functions.
- **Judicious use of select** Provides clear menu-driven user input.

Beyond case: Other Conditional Constructs

Remember, while powerful, the `case` statement focuses on pattern matching. Bash offers several more:

- **`if/elif/else` Blocks:** Best for complex comparisons, boolean logic (`-eq`, `-lt`, etc. are your tools here)
- **Test (`[  ]` and `[[  ]]`):** Often used within `if` conditions. [[https://tldp.org/LDP/abs/html/testconstructs.html]] for details.

Additional Resources

- **Regular Expressions** https://www.regular-expressions.info/ (Used lightly here, a powerful topic in its own right!)
- **Advanced Bash Scripting Guide: Nested Case Statements** https://www.tldp.org/LDP/abs/html/nestedloops.html

Crafting Intelligent Scripts

These techniques bring nuanced decision-making to your scripts, increasing their ability to handle complexity.

Next on our agenda: Effective logging strategies to understand the internal state of your running scripts! Let me know when you're ready.

Section 6:
Effective Logging Strategies

Introduction to Script Logging Techniques

Scripts, once running, often become silent black boxes. Logging lets them communicate their status, what they're doing, and most importantly, where things go wrong. It creates an essential trail for both live monitoring and later troubleshooting.

Why Logging Matters

- **Understanding Execution:** Seeing a script's step-by-step progress offers deeper understanding than just success/failure.
- **Troubleshooting:** When something fails, logs are your most powerful diagnostic tool to pinpoint the problem.
- **Auditing:** For critical processes, logs are a record of actions, useful for both security and compliance reasons.
- **Tracking Changes:** Over time, they are a 'history' of what happened on a system due to your scripts.

Basic Bash Logging: Redirections

You already know the fundamentals! Here's how to start immediately:

- **Output to a File:**

```
my_script.sh > /var/log/my_script.log
```

- **Append to File:**

```
echo "Script task completed" >>
/var/log/my_script.log
```

- **Errors Only (2>)**

```
some_command 2> errors.log
```

Best Practices (Even Early On)

- **Timestamps:** Log entries become most meaningful with timestamps. You can craft this manually:

```
timestamp=$(date "+%Y-%m-%d %H:%M:%S")
echo "$timestamp - Backup Started" >> backup.log
```

- **Dedicated Log Files:** Avoid mixing your output in existing system logs. Give your scripts their own logging space.

Introducing logger

This command-line tool standardizes sending messages to your system's logging facility (syslogd on most Linux systems).

```
logger -t my_script "Starting data import
process"  # '-t' adds a tag
```

- **Benefit:** Your system likely has log rotation to prevent files from growing endlessly, and tools to filter your script's logs specifically.

Levels of Logging

As scripts get complex, log different severities:

- **Info:** Progress updates, successful steps
- **Warning:** Errors that were *recovered* from, unexpected situations
- **Error:** Something's failed. The script might halt or try to limp along.
- **Debug:** Verbose output (may involve sensitive data), often enabled temporarily

Example: Enhanced Backup Script

```
log_file="/var/log/my_backup.log"

log_info() {
    echo "$(date '+%Y-%m-%d %H:%M:%S') INFO: $1"
>> $log_file
}

log_warning() {
    echo "$(date '+%Y-%m-%d %H:%M:%S') WARN: $1"
>> $log_file
}
# .... similarly for log_error, log_debug

log_info "Backup initiated"
# ..... backup steps....
```

Additional Resources

- **Linux Logging Basics - Syslog, rsyslog, Journald:**
  https://linux-audit.com/linux-logging-basics/
- **The logger command on Linux**
  https://man7.org/linux/man-pages/man1/logger.1.html

Next Up: Going Pro

In "Advanced Logging: Methods and Best Practices", we'll cover customizing log formats, leveraging your system's log facilities, and strategies for large-scale log management.

Advanced Logging: Methods and Best Practices

You understand the why and basics of logging. Now, let's explore how to integrate logging expertly into your scripts for maximum clarity and efficiency.

Beyond Simple Files: Syslog

Most Linux systems have a logging daemon (`rsyslogd` or `syslog-ng`) configured to:

- **Categorize Logs:** Messages tagged with facilities (`auth`, `cron`, `user`, etc.) and severity levels (`info`, `warn`, `crit`)
- **Route Log Traffic:** To different files, network targets, even databases.

Using `logger` Effectively

1. **Set Message Priority:**

```
logger -p user.notice "Script initiated archival process"
```

See `man logger` for priority levels.

2. **Tagging (Important!):**

```
logger -t disk_cleanup -s "Cleaned 10.5GB of old log files"
 # '-s' also prints to STDOUT, great for live status display
```

Tags give you log filters to see *just* your script's output

Centralized Logging

For multiple machines, send logs over the network:

- **Remote Syslog Server:** Can receive messages over UDP, TCP (reliable, use for mission-critical stuff). Your `rsyslog` config defines which messages it accepts.
- **ELK/EFK or Graylog:** Popular log aggregation platforms. Great when lots of different sources need management, analysis, and dashboards.

Log Rotation with 'logrotate'

Unmanaged log files become a problem! 'logrotate' is your companion:

- **Daily, Weekly, Size-based Rotation:** Prevents growth into gigabytes
- **Compression:** Old logs take up less space
- **Retention Control:** Auto-discard very old logs

Example 'logrotate' config snippet for your Script:

```
/var/log/my_script.log {
    daily
    rotate 14   # Keep 2 weeks of history
    compress
    missingok   # No fuss if the log file isn't there yet
}
```

Structured Logging (Enter JSON)

- **What:** Instead of just lines, log entries as JSON objects:
  { "timestamp": "2023-07-30T20:20:41Z", "severity": "INFO", "message": "Backup successful", "file_count": 38 }
- **Why:**

- ○ Machine readable; easily parsed for analysis and dashboards.
- ○ Add as many key-value pairs as you need!
- **Generating JSON in Bash** Requires tools like 'jq': https://stedolan.github.io/jq/ (beyond the scope of this chapter, but powerful).

Logging Best Practices

- **Consistency is Key:** Standard formats/loglevels make everything much easier to work with.
- **Don't Log Secrets:** Credentials or sensitive data in log files is a huge security risk.
- **Balance Verbosity:** Too much is as bad as too little. Log at the level matching your use-case:
  - ○ Debugging – lots of detail, temporarily enabled
  - ○ Production – less noise, but capture meaningful state
- **Test:** Your logging setup *before* going live. Check your syslog config, that logrotate works, etc.

Additional Resources

- **rsyslog Configuration guide:** https://www.rsyslog.com/doc/v8-stable/
- **Structured Logging:** https://stackify.com/what-is-structured-logging-and-why-developers-need-it/

Smart Logging = Happy Admins (and future you!)

Logs become your historical reference, allowing you to understand past behavior or failures of your scripts.

Next up, we'll start our discussion on "Looping Mechanisms: The While Loop," giving your scripts the ability to act repetitively based on conditions.

Section 7:

Looping Mechanisms:

The While Loop

Fundamentals of While Loops in Scripts

Scripts often need to perform the same task multiple times until a condition is met. The while loop is your workhorse, automating tasks to a degree straight-line scripts simply can't.

The Logic of the while Loop

1. **A Condition Is Tested:** This is like a mini if statement at the top of the loop.
2. **A Code Block:** If the condition is **true**, the code within this block executes.
3. **Back to the Top:** After the code block, the loop jumps back to the start, reevaluating the condition. This continues until the condition becomes **false**.

Basic Structure

```
while [ condition ]; do
    # Code to execute while the condition is true
done
```

Example #1: Countdown

```
counter=5
while [ $counter -gt 0 ]; do
    echo "Countdown: $counter"
    counter=$(( counter - 1 ))   # Decrement
counter
done
echo "Liftoff!"
```

Important Concepts

- **The Test Condition:** Inside the [ ] can be any command or expression that can evaluate to true or false. Often, comparisons (-gt, -lt, -eq, etc.) are used.
- **Changing the Condition:** Something *inside* your loop's code block **must** make the condition eventually become false, or you'll have an infinite loop (bad)!
- **Using External Commands:** Your loop's condition can depend on a program call:

```
while ! ping -c1 google.com > /dev/null; do   #
Repeat until 'ping' succeeds
    echo "Waiting for internet connection..."
    sleep 5
done
```

Practical Applications

1. **Processing Files in a Directory:**

```
for file in *.txt; do
    while read line; do
        # Process each line of the file
    done < "$file"
```

```
done
```

2. User Input Validation

```
while true; do  # Use 'break' to exit within the loop
    read -p "Enter a number greater than 10: " number
    if [ $number -gt 10 ]; then
        break
    fi
    echo "Invalid input, please try again."
done
```

3. Monitoring

```
while :  # ':' is always true - use with care!
do
    disk_usage=$(df -h / | awk '{print $5}' | tail -n1 | cut -d '%' -f 1)
    if [ $disk_usage -gt 85 ]; then
        echo "Low disk space alert!" | mail -s "Disk Warning" admin@example.com
    fi
    sleep 300  # Check every 5 minutes
done
```

Additional Resources

- **While Loop Explainer:**
  http://tldp.org/LDP/Bash-Beginners-Guide/html/sect_09_02.html
- **GNU Bash Manual - While Loops:**
  https://www.gnu.org/software/bash/manual/html_node/Bash-Conditional-Expressions.html

Cautions

- **Watch Those Infinite Loops:** Always ensure your loops terminate. Test carefully, especially before putting monitoring loops into production.
- **Nested Loops:** When while loops are placed inside each other, ensure your logic for managing conditions avoids unexpected hangs.

Next: Making while Dance

In the next chapter, "Complex Applications of While Loops", we'll explore while with file reading, prompts, and calculated conditions for greater scripting power.

Complex Applications of While Loops

You've grasped the essence of the `while` loop. Now, let's see how its simple structure can orchestrate surprisingly intricate behavior with a few additional techniques.

Reading Files Line-by-Line

Using a `while` `read` loop is the idiomatic way to process text files in Bash:

```
while read -r line; do
    echo "Processing line: $line"
done < input_file.txt
```

- **Explained:**
    - `read -r line` reads each line of 'input_file.txt' into the variable $line
    - The loop implicitly ends when there are no more lines.
    - It's better than `cat file.txt | while...` (avoid those extra processes!)

Example: CSV Processing

```
while IFS=, read -r name email phone; do
    echo "Name: $name, Email: $email"
done < contacts.csv
```

- **IFS=',':** Sets the field separator to a comma for CSV handling.

Prompts with Validation

```
while true; do
    read -p "Please enter your password: "
password
    if [[ ${#password} -ge 8 && "$password" =~
[A-Z] && "$password" =~ [0-9] ]]; then
        echo "Strong password accepted."
        break  # Password meets our criteria
    else
        echo "Password must be at least 8
characters, with uppercase and digits."
    fi
done
```

- **[[...]]:** Enhanced test construct for things like string length (-ge 8) and regular expression matching (=~)
- **Infinite Loop on Purpose:** Here, the break within the loop provides the controlled exit when conditions are met.

Monitoring with 'sleep'

```
while true; do
    if ps -ef | grep -q
"my_long_running_process.py"; then
        echo "$(date) - Process is running"
    else
        echo "$(date) - Process has stopped!
Sending alert..."
        # ... Your notification actions here ...
    fi
    sleep 60  # Check every minute
done
```

- **ps -ef | grep:** Crude, but illustrates checking whether a process exists.

- **Infinite Loop (Carefully!):** For monitors, it's common to `sleep` and loop indefinitely unless you have a defined endpoint.

Calculated Conditions

```
attempts=0
until [ $attempts -ge 5 ]; do  # 'until' is like
'while' but the logic is inverted
    rsync -avz /data/ remote_host:/backup/
    if [ $? -eq 0 ]; then
        echo "Backup successful!"
        break
    fi
    attempts=$(( attempts + 1 ))
    echo "Backup failed. Retrying. (Attempt
$attempts of 5)"
    sleep 30
done
```

- **Until:** The loop body runs while the condition remains **false**. Great for retry logic.

Important Notes

- **File Descriptors:** When processing large input files using `while read`, extra attention might be needed. (Search 'Bash while read large files')
- **External Factors:** Loop complexity heavily depends on the commands you use within and how their success/failure is tested.

Additional Resources

- **Until Loops in Bash:**
  http://tldp.org/LDP/Bash-Beginners-Guide/html/sect_09_06.html

The Limits of a `while` Loop

- Pure math loops are often done better with `for` (we'll cover those soon)
- Very complex, nested decision-making within `while` might be clearer with functions and `if`/`else`. It's all about which style keeps your code understandable!

Section 8:
Strategies for Debugging Bash Scripts

Basic Debugging Techniques

The best developers aren't those who don't write bugs, but the ones who find and fix them efficiently. Let's start building your detective skills for script troubleshooting.

The Mindset: Script As Hypothesis

Remember, script execution is your experiment. If you don't get the expected result, figure out *where* your logic or assumptions diverge from reality.

Technique 1: echo Statements

The workhorse of simple debugging! Insert echo at various points:

- **Checking Variable Values:**

```
echo "Script started. Input file is: $input_file"
```

- **Tracing Execution Flow**

```
echo "Entering download function..."
echo "Download complete, processing data..."
```

Technique 2: Running with bash -x

Turns on step-by-step tracing of your script:

```
bash -x my_script.sh
```

- **The Output:** Each line is prefixed with a + followed by the expanded and executed result. Extremely useful for seeing variables, mismatched wildcards, etc.

Technique 3: Subshells for Isolation

```
(
    cd temporary_workspace
    # Commands that might affect your main
script's environment
)
```

- **Why:** Sometimes you need to debug code that modifies files, directories, or variables – subshells (( )) create a clean sandbox for testing. Changes inside aren't permanent.

Technique 4: Redirecting Errors (2>&1)

Capture errors while tracing with bash -x:

```
bash -x my_script.sh  2>&1 | tee debug_output.txt
```

- **Understanding:**
    - 2>&1 sends error output (file descriptor 2) to the same place as standard output (file descriptor 1).
    - tee lets you see the output in the console *and* saves it to 'debug_output.txt' for analysis.

Example: Debugging File Processing

```
#!/bin/bash
set -x  # Activate tracing from here onwards
```

```
for file in *.csv; do
    echo "Processing: $file"
    new_filename=$(echo $file | sed
's/.csv/_report.txt/')
    process_data "$file" > "$new_filename"
done.
```

Strategic Debugging

- **Incremental:** Don't add 'echo' everywhere; target suspicious areas.
- **Clean Up:** Remove debugging code later!
- **Error Messages are Clues:** Often, a command's error message will directly provide the information needed to fix the issue with your input or parameters.

Additional Resources

- **Linux Journal: Bash Debugging**
  https://www.linuxjournal.com/content/bash-debugging
- **Bash Hackers Wiki: Debugging**
  http://wiki.bash-hackers.org/scripting/debuggingtips

Things Get Even More Interesting…

Basic debugging is about observation. Up next, in "Intermediate Debugging Strategies," we'll look at ways to interactively modify your script while it's running and examine it on a deeper level.

Intermediate Debugging Strategies

You've mastered the core debugging techniques; now, let's get more interactive and go beyond just observing your script's behavior.

Technique 1: Setting Breakpoints with trap

trap lets you "catch" signals and execute code during your script's run:

```
function debug_trap() {
   set -x  # Turn on tracing
   echo "Paused at line: $LINENO, in function
'$BASH_COMMAND'"
   read -p "Enter 'c' to continue, 's' to step,
or commands: " action
   case "$action" in
      c) set +x ;;  # Continue, turn off tracing
      s) : ;;       # Single step (use
repeatedly)
      *) bash -c "$action"  # Execute other
debugging commands
   esac
}

trap debug_trap DEBUG
```

- **How to Use It:**
  1. Insert the debug_trap function into your script.
  2. Trigger breakpoint-like behavior by sending the DEBUG signal at a certain point.

a. Manually with: `kill -s DEBUG $$` (where $$ is the script's process ID)
 b. Or within the script via a well-placed `kill -s DEBUG $$` (carefully!)

- **In the Trap:** You have a mini-shell: examine variables, execute commands for manual checks, etc.

Technique 2: Selective Execution

Sometimes, you need to isolate a misbehaving section:

1. **Comment Out Blocks:** Suspect a function? Comment it out temporarily.
2. **Simplify Input:** If data-driven, provide a minimal input file for testing.
3. **Hardcode Values:** Temporarily bypass variables, providing the data your code block expects directly to see if the processing itself is the culprit.

Technique 3: The `sleep` Command

Crude, but remarkably useful in a few situations:

- **Slowing Things Down:** Script running too fast to follow? Add `sleep 1` or `sleep 2` to see intermediate changes.
- **Waiting for External Resources:** Need a file to appear that another process generates? A loop with `sleep` before retrying is common practice.

Technique 4: Advanced echo Tricks

- **Show variable state:** `echo "Value of x = $x (before the loop)"`
- **Fancy Formatting:**

```
echo "------------------- START OF SECTION
------------------"
```

Debugging Best Practices

- **Test Incrementally:** Write code in small, easy-to-test units (functions help!)
- **Version Control:** (e.g., Git) Allows you to quickly compare a failing version of your script against an earlier working one.
- **"Rubber Duck Debugging"** https://blog.codinghorror.com/rubber-duck-problem-solving/: Explaining your code out loud, even to an inanimate object, often makes the problem jump out at you!

Additional Resources

- **GreyCat Wiki: Debugging Bash Scripts** http://mywiki.wooledge.org/BashGuide/Debugging

When It Gets Complex

Even intermediate techniques run out of steam with very complex scripts. That's why, in "Advanced Debugging Methods", we'll cover dedicated debuggers like bashdb which provide even greater introspection.

Advanced Debugging Methods

When echo and trap just don't cut it anymore, it's time for the serious artillery. Let's equip you with techniques worthy of the trickiest bugs.

Prerequisite: Recompiling Bash (If Desired)

Some distributions compile Bash in a mode limiting the effectiveness of the built-in debugger. If you intend to use bashdb to its full potential, you might need to recompile Bash from source with debug flags enabled.

Technique 1: The Bash Debugger (bashdb)

Not as fancy as visual debuggers in IDEs, but surprisingly powerful. bashdb is a command-line debugger specialized for Bash.

1. **Running Your Script:**
   - bashdb my_script.sh
   - If already running, attach to the process with bashdb <pid_of_script>
2. **Inside the Debugger:** (Here's a small subset of available commands)
   - list: Show your script's source code around the current execution point.
   - step: Advance one line of code (steps into functions).
   - next: Advance one line, but skip stepping into functions.
   - print <variable_name>: Examine a variable's value.

    ○ `break <line_number>`: Set a breakpoint to pause execution.

    ○ `cont`: Continue running after a pause.

    ○ `help`: See the full command list.

Example Workflow

1. Identify a general area where the bug might be lurking.
2. Set a breakpoint near the start of that area.
3. Use 'step' and 'next' to execute in slow motion, 'print' variables, and watch your script state evolve.

Technique 2: Enhanced Tracing with `set` Options

- `set -v:` Prints each line of your script *before* execution (raw text, unexpanded).
- `set -x:` (You know this one!) Prints lines *after* variable expansion etc., giving more runtime insight than '-v'.

When Not to Use Them:

- **Production Systems:** Debuggers and tracing have performance impacts. Avoid running with these in a production environment.
- **Simple Errors:** Overkill for typos or basic variable checks.

Technique 3: External Linters

Linters analyze code for style issues, but also potential errors!

- **ShellCheck:** The gold standard Bash linter. Catches many common mistakes.
  - Online version: https://www.shellcheck.net/
  - Can be integrated into many text editors, giving you early error warnings as you write.

Debugging Requires Patience

These advanced tools open new frontiers, but the debugging mindset remains important:

- **Hypothesize:** Come up with possible explanations about *why* it's wrong.
- **Experiment:** Change code/input, look for patterns of failure vs. success.
- **Isolate:** Zero in on the smallest misbehaving unit using breakpoints or by commenting chunks of code.

Additional Resources

- **GNU Bash Manual - Bash Debugger**
  https://www.gnu.org/software/bash/manual/html_node/The-Set-Builtin.html#The-Set-Builtin
- **ShellCheck Website:** https://www.shellcheck.net/

Expert Debugging

We won't leave you here unarmed! The final chapter in our debugging section, "Expert Tips for Efficient Debugging", will cover how to become a bug fixing ninja with real-world advice and workflow considerations.

Expert Tips for Efficient Debugging

By now, you have an arsenal of debugging tools. Let's solidify this with strategies to streamline your bug hunting – saving time and sanity!

Prevention is Better Than Cure

- **Defensive Programming:** Assume user input may be wrong, files might be missing. Handle errors gracefully *within* your scripts, with messages guiding a solution.
- **Modularity:** Small, single-purpose functions are easier to test in isolation than giant monolithic scripts.
- **Logging:** Even basic logs act as 'breadcrumbs' during a script's execution.

When Things Go Wrong...

- **Don't Panic:** Bugs happen to everyone. Hasty, random changes often make it worse.
- **Gather Data:** What *exactly* is wrong? Error messages, logs, even recent system changes all can provide clues.
- **Reproducibility:** If you can reliably make the bug happen, you're well on your way to understanding its trigger.

Workflow Tactics

- **Rubber Duck It:** Seriously! Explain the problem out loud – as if to someone (or an inanimate object) who knows nothing about your code. The process sparks connections.
- **Take Notes:** Jotting down variable values, function call order, or your working theories allows you to spot patterns

- **Sleep on It:** Frustrated after intense debugging? Sometimes, walking away gives your subconscious a chance to assemble the puzzle.

Mental Models Matter

- **"Impossible" Bugs:** They usually reveal a misunderstanding about your scripts environment, tools, or assumptions. These are a valuable learning opportunity!
- **The Scientific Method:** This applies to coding too! Hypothesize, test, revise your hypothesis. Stay systematic.
- **Ask for Help:** Fresh eyes work wonders. Forums, colleagues – sometimes all it takes is explaining your logic to unveil the problem.

Pro Tips

- **Version Control:** Being able to see the difference between when it worked and now is debugging gold.
- **Pair Debugging:** Two developers tackling a problem. One person explains the code, the other looks for inconsistencies and asks questions.
- **"Binary Search" Debugging:** Comment out half your code, see if the problem is still there. Repeat this halving-down to zero in. Works better with somewhat modular scripts.

Debugging as a Skill

With each conquered bug, you get better at:

1. **Pattern Recognition:** Bugs often reoccur in new disguises. You gain experience anticipating problems.
2. **Intuition:** That subtle 'hmm, this feels wrong' sense will develop, steering you towards faulty areas even before errors surface.

Additional Resources

- **Debugging Faqs (General Programming)**
  https://stackoverflow.com/questions/tagged/debugging
- **The Pragmatic Programmer Book** (Excellent chapter on debugging mindset)
  https://pragprog.com/titles/tpp20/the-pragmatic-programmer-20th-anniversary-edition/

Beyond Code-Level Bugs

While we've focused on debugging your script, always remember – system configuration, external services, hardware… the fault may lie elsewhere! This is where system-wide logs and a broader understanding of IT are as important as Bash skills.

Happy Bug Hunting!

Debugging shouldn't be feared. Mastering these techniques brings a rewarding feeling of understanding and control over your code creations.

Section 9:
Transforming Data and Text with Sed

Introduction to Sed for Data Manipulation

While born for editing, the core essence of 'sed' is pattern-based action. This is a superpower for cleaning, restructuring, and extracting the information you need from the raw text files often encountered during scripting and system administration.

What 'sed' Is (And Isn't)

- **Stream Editor:** It takes input (from a file or piped in), processes lines sequentially according to your sed script, and sends the result to output.
- **Not an In-place Editor:** 'sed' *by default* doesn't directly modify your files. Learn the techniques to apply changes back safely a little later.
- **Not a Full Programming Language:** Its operations are focused on text manipulation, lacking the complex data structures or 'traditional' features you'd associate with Python, etc.

Basic Structure of a sed Command

```
sed 'script' input_file
```

- **The 'script' Part:**
  - ○ Contains addresses (selecting which lines to act on) and commands (what to do on those lines).
  - ○ Can be directly on the command line or in a separate .sed file for larger scripts.

Our Playground: Sample File ('data.txt')

Let's imagine this represents, say, system logs:

ERROR: Application failed to start [Code 127]
INFO: Web server listening on port 80
WARNING: Security update required (CVE-2023-21298)

Command #1: Basic Substitution

```
sed 's/ERROR/ALERT/' data.txt
```

- **Explained:**
  - ○ s/old/new/: The universal 'substitute' command
  - ○ This outputs our file with 'ERROR' changed to 'ALERT'
- **Note:** data.txt remains unchanged!

Command #2: Addresses for Selective Editing

```
sed '/WARNING/ s/required/urgent/' data.txt
```

- **The Address Part:** /WARNING/ limits the substitution *only* to lines containing the word 'WARNING'.
- **Output:** Other lines are now passed through unmodified.

Command #3: Deleting Lines

```
sed '/^INFO/d' data.txt
```

- **d is for delete:** The address /^INFO/ matches lines starting with 'INFO'
- **Output:** Our 'INFO' line vanishes; error messages remain.

Important Principles

- **Regular Expressions:** 'sed' uses them for sophisticated matching (beyond what we'll show today, a deep topic!)
- **Chaining:** Complex transformations often result from multiple 'sed' commands piped together.
- **Safe Editing:** Test with an output redirect first (sed ... > new_file), or make a backup of your data!

Up Next

Now you have the base tools. In "Intermediate Techniques in Sed", we'll unlock more commands, address ranges, and how to make those file changes "stick"!

Intermediate Techniques in Sed

You've grasped 'sed' fundamentals. Now, prepare for a power-up as we tackle more advanced ways to select lines, combine commands, and even do a bit of pseudo-calculation!

Addressing Techniques

- **Line Numbers:**

```
sed '3d' data.txt  #  Deletes the 3rd line
```

- **Ranges:**

```
sed '1,5 s/\[.*\]//g' data.txt  # Removes [Code 127]-like parts from lines 1 to 5
```

- **Multiple Matches:** /ERROR/,/WARNING/ (An address from pattern 'ERROR' to the subsequent 'WARNING')

Command Deep Dives

- **'g' Flag for Global Replace:**

```
sed 's/:/;/g' data.txt  # Replaces *all* colons with semicolons in each line
```

- **Numbered Replacements:**

```
sed 's/\([0-9]\{3\}\)-\([0-9]\{4\}\)/(\2) \1/'
phone_data.txt
```

   - Uses capture groups ( ) and backreferences (\1, \2) to reformat phone numbers!

- **The 'y' Command (Translation):**

```
sed 'y/abc/XYZ/' data.txt  # Replaces each 'a' ->
'X', 'b' -> 'Y', etc.
```

Saving Changes - The '-i' Option

- **Use with Caution:** `sed -i 's/foo/bar/g'`
  `my_file.txt` edits the file directly
- **Backups First:** `sed -i.bak 's/foo/bar/g'`
  `my_file.txt` is safer (creates my_file.txt.bak)

Multi-Command 'sed' Scripts

```
sed -e 's/ERROR/CRITICAL/g'  \
    -e '/Code/d' data.txt
```

- `-e` is for specifying multiple commands
- Each line is basically a mini 'sed' program on its own. Order matters!

Example: Complex Substitution

```
sed '/<title>/,/<\/title>/ {  # Operate within
<title> tags
        s/Old Title/My New Title/
    }' index.html
```

Sed in Your Scripts

1. **Inline:**

```
new_filename=$(echo $old_filename | sed
's/\.txt/_final.log/')
```

2. Temporary Storage:

```
sed '...' data.txt > tmp_file
# Do more processing on 'tmp_file'
```

Additional Resources

- **Sed: An Introduction and Tutorial:**
  https://www.grymoire.com/Unix/Sed.html
- **The 'awk' Command:** A fellow text-processing master with
  a different focus:
  https://www.gnu.org/software/gawk/manual/gawk.html

Practice Makes Perfect

Find small text files (code, configs, etc.) and experiment! 'sed' lets
you quickly ask "what if I changed these…" without affecting the
source.

Advanced Text Transformations Using Sed

In the previous chapters on Sed, you gained a solid grasp of its fundamentals and intermediate capabilities. Now, we'll elevate your skills and explore the more sophisticated text transformations achievable using this powerful stream editor.

Harnessing Hold Space and Exchange Commands

- **The Hold Space:** Think of Sed's hold space as a temporary storage area. Commands like 'h' (copy pattern space to hold space) and 'H' (append pattern space to hold space) let you strategically preserve text for later use.
- **The Exchange Command ('x'):** The 'x' command swaps the contents of the pattern space and the hold space. This lets you retrieve stored lines for intricate manipulations.

Example: Reversing Lines

Consider a file 'lines.txt':

Line one

Line two

Line three

We can reverse the order of the lines with the following sed script:

```
sed -n '1!G;h;$p' lines.txt
```

Explanation:

1. -n: Suppresses default output.
2. 1!G: For all lines except the first, append the hold space to the pattern space (with a newline inserted between).
3. h: Copy the pattern space (multiple lines now) to the hold space.
4. $p: On the last line, print the pattern space (which now contains the reversed lines).

Advanced Pattern Matching with Regular Expressions

- **Backreferences:** Backreferences let you reuse portions of a matched pattern within your replacement text. Use '\1', '\2', etc. to refer to captured groups in parentheses.

Example: Swapping Words

```
sed 's/\(.*\) \([^ ]*\)/\2 \1/'
```

This swaps the first and second words on each line.

- **Extended Regular Expressions (ERE):** Enable ERE with the '-r' flag for a simplified syntax within patterns (e.g., using '?', '+', and '|' without escaping).

Example: Selective Deletion

```
sed -r '/^(Apple|Orange)/d' fruits.txt
```

Removes lines starting with "Apple" or "Orange".

Complex Multi-Command Sed Scripts

Combine multiple Sed commands using either semicolons (;) for one-liners or curly braces '{}' for more readable multi-line scripts.

Example: Multi-Step Modification

```
sed -e 's/OldText/NewText/g' -e
'/SpecificPattern/d' input.txt
```

1. Replaces "OldText" with "NewText" globally.
2. Deletes lines matching "SpecificPattern".

Branching and Conditional Execution

- **Branching with 'b' and 't':** Implement conditional logic in Sed scripts:
    - 'b [label]' : Branch unconditionally to a label.
    - 't [label]' : Branch to a label only if a substitution has been successful.

Example: Conditional Replacement

```
sed '

/SearchTerm/ {

  s/Old/New/  # Perform replacement if
'SearchTerm' is found

  t           # Jump to end if substitution
occurred

}

:end        # Label to jump to

'
```

In-Place File Editing

Use the '-i' option for in-place file modification. **Caution:** Always work on a backup copy first!

```
sed -i 's/original/replacement/g' your_file.txt
```

Resources

- **GNU Sed Manual:**
  https://www.gnu.org/software/sed/manual/sed.html
- **Regular Expressions Info:**
  https://www.regular-expressions.info/
- **Grymoire's Sed Tutorial:**
  https://www.grymoire.com/Unix/Sed.html

Expert Level Data Manipulation with Sed

In previous chapters, you've mastered Sed's core functionality and discovered its sophisticated text transformation capabilities. This chapter unlocks the true power of Sed for expert-tier data manipulation tasks often approaching what you might think requires a full-fledged programming language.

Sed as a Mini-Programming Language

While Sed is primarily a stream editor, its features make it surprisingly capable of intricate data manipulation resembling code:

- **Hold Space:** A temporary buffer for complex text juggling.
- **Branching and labels:** Implement if-then-like logic.
- **Regular Expressions:** Powerful pattern matching for selective manipulation.

Scenario 1: CSV Parsing and Transformation

Sed can excel where simple tools like 'cut' fall short. Let's parse a CSV file ('data.csv'):

```
name,age,city
Alice,30,New York
Bob,25,Chicago
```

- **Task: Create an HTML Table**

```
sed -e '1s/^/<table>\n/' -e 's/,/<td>/g' -e
'$a</table>' -e 's/.*/<tr><td>&<\/td><\/tr>/'
data.csv
```

Explanation

1. First line - Inserts the HTML table opening tag (<table>).
2. Replace commas with table cell delimiters (<td></td>).
3.).Last line - Appends the table closing tag (</table>).
4. Wrap each line in table row elements (<tr><td>...</td></tr>

Scenario 2: Complex Pattern-Based Extraction

Let's extract key-value pairs from an 'ini' style config file:

```
[Server]
host=webserver.com
port=8080
[Database]
username=admin
```

- **Task: Get 'host' and 'username'**

```
sed -nr '/^\[(\w+)\]/{N;s/^host=(.*)/Server Host: \1/;s/^username=(.*)/DB User: \1/;p}' config.ini
```

Explanation:

- -n: Suppress regular output.
- -r: Enable extended regular expressions.
- /^\[(\w+)\]/: Match section headers, capture the name ('Server', 'Database').
- N: Append the next line to the pattern space.
- Substitution commands search for 'host=' and 'username=' lines, extracting those values and creating formatted output.

Scenario 3: Emulating Multi-Stage Filtering

Sed's hold space makes it possible to process text over multiple passes:

- **Task:** Reverse lines within a file *only* between markers 'START' and 'END'.

```
sed -n '/START/{h;d;};/END/{G;};p'  file.txt
```

Explanation

1. `/START/{h;d;}`: On 'START', copy the line to hold space, delete from pattern space (skip to next line).
2. `/END/{G;}`: On 'END', append the hold space to the pattern space.
3. p: Default print of pattern space (reversed lines in marked section).

Limitations of Sed

- **Complex numerical calculations:** For heavy math, tools like 'awk' are often better suited.
- **Large Data Structures:** If you need arrays, dictionaries, etc., a traditional programming language would be necessary.

Advanced Tips

- **Experiment:** Sed excels with practice. Test it with small datasets.
- **Comment your Sed scripts:** Complex Sed can become obscure. Use '#' for comments within your scripts.
- **Break problems into steps:** Large transformations are easier when broken down into smaller Sed commands.

Resources

- **The Sed FAQ:** https://www.gnu.org/software/sed/manual/html_node/FAQ.html

- **Sed One-Liners Explained:**
  https://github.com/learnbyexample/learn_gnused

Creative Applications of Sed in Scripting

Sed's ability to manipulate text often inspires unconventional problem-solving approaches. Let's dive into examples that blur the lines between pure text editing and mini-programs!

Scenario 1: Self-Modifying Scripts

While it requires caution, Sed can modify its *own* script file for dynamic behavior.

Example: A Usage Counter

```
#!/bin/bash

sed -i '1s/^/count=$((count+1))\n/' "$0"  # Increment a counter on each run

echo "This script has been run $count times."

# ...rest of the script's logic
```

Explanation:

- **Caution:** It's generally safer to modify a *copy* of a script. Errors could make the script unrunnable.
- "$0" : Refers to the filename of the script itself.
- The substitution inserts a line at the beginning, incrementing a count variable.

Scenario 2: In-Script Configuration

Store simple configuration values within comments in your script, extractable by Sed:

```
#!/bin/bash

# #CONFIG: email=someone@example.com

# ...

email=$(sed -n 's/^# #CONFIG: email=\(.*\)/\1/p'
"$0")

echo "Sending report to $email"
```

Advantages:

- Configuration bundled with the script itself.
- Easily adjustable without complex config file formats.

Scenario 3: Selective Code Execution

Implement basic code toggling via Sed:

```
#!/bin/bash

# ...some code

sed '/## DEBUG START/,/## DEBUG END/{///!d;}' "$0"
| bash

# ... more code
```

- Code sections between "DEBUG START" and "DEBUG END" will be conditionally executed.
- Works because Sed, by default, doesn't modify lines starting with '##'. The /!d flips this to *only* process and run those debug lines.

Scenario 4: Ad-hoc Code Generation

Sed can generate Bash code fragments as output for dynamic script creation.

Example: Array Population

```
data="item1 item2 item3"

 sed -e "s/\s/\"\);\n/g; s/.*/array=(\&/;
1s/^/array=("/" <<< "$data"
```

This outputs:

array=("item1");

array=("item2");

array=("item3");

…which defines a Bash array, useful for building a more complex script from data input.

Scenario 5: Lightweight Templating

While limited compared to true templating, Sed can do basic variable substitution.

```
template='Hello, NAME! The current date is DATE'

name="Alice"

date=$(date)

sed "s/NAME/$name/g; s/DATE/$date/g" <<<
"$template"
```

Notes on Creativity

- **Balance with readability:** Clever can become cryptic – use comments!
- **Don't force it:** If a task grows too complex for Sed, a little Python or Perl code might be cleaner.

- **Inspiration from others:** Search for "creative Sed uses" online for unusual ideas.

Resources

- **Obscure Sed One-liners:** Sometimes "crazy" reveals new tricks https://github.com/veltman/sed1line
- **Stack Overflow - 'Sed' tag:** Look for real-world problem solving https://stackoverflow.com/questions/tagged/sed

Sed Mastery: Complex Use Cases and Scenarios

By now, you have a powerful command over Sed's fundamentals and its more advanced applications. In this chapter, we'll combine these techniques to tackle intricate scenarios that demonstrate the extent of Sed's problem-solving abilities.

Scenario 1: Refactoring Log Files

Log files often have inconsistent formats. Sed can unify them. Let's transform an Apache-style log ('access.log'):

1.2.3.4 - - [01/Feb/2023:10:25:16] "GET /images/logo.png HTTP/1.1" 200 2550

...into a CSV-like format:

2023-02-01,10:25:16,1.2.3.4,/images/logo.png,200,2550

Sed Script:

```
sed -r '
    s/ - - \[(.*)\] "(.*) HTTP\/1.1" (\d+)
(\d+)$/\1,\2,\3,\4/

s/([0-9]{2})\/([A-Za-z]+)\/([0-9]{4}):/\3-\2-\1,/
' access.log
```

Explanation:

- **-r:** Enables extended regular expressions for simpler syntax.
- **Multiple substitutions:** Each 's/.../.../' command transforms a portion of the log format.

- **Complex capturing:** Parentheses are used extensively to capture relevant log portions.
- **Backreferences:** Rearranges log components into the target format (\1, \2, etc.).

Scenario 2: In-Place Code Modification

Sometimes you need to alter embedded patterns within source code files. For example, let's update version numbers in a configuration file ('config.py'):

```
version_string = "0.3.7"
# ... some more code
```

Sed Script:

```
sed -i -r 's/(version_string =
")(\d+\.\d+\.)(\d+)("\s*)/\1\2\3\4/' config.py
```

Explanation:

- **-i** Edit in-place (Caution: operate on a backup first!)
- **Selective editing:** The pattern ensures we only change the 'version_string' line.
- **Incrementing digits:** The (\d+) portion captures the last digit, allowing it to be incremented using backreferences (calculated substitution is beyond Sed's usual realm).

Scenario 3: Website Mirroring (Basic)

Sed can help fetch basic website structures, with some limitations.

```
curl -s https://example.com/ | sed -n
's/.*href="\([^"]*\).*/\1/p' |
 while read link; do
  curl -s "https://example.com/$link" >
"${link//\//.}"
 done
```

Caution: Complex sites will fail due to JavaScript, relative linking, etc.

Explanation:

- **Initial Fetch:** 'curl' gets the initial HTML
- **Sed extracts links:** Sed isolates only the URLs enclosed within 'href="…"' attributes.
- **Looping and Download:** A 'while' loop reads Sed's output, using 'curl' to fetch each 'link'. Filenames are slightly sanitized for safety.

Mastery Tips

- **Practice on varied data:** Test your Sed skills on diverse text formats to strengthen pattern matching.
- **Don't fear long Sed scripts:** Complex problems might require chaining many substitution and editing commands together.
- **Build tools incrementally:** Develop Sed solutions step by step, testing each addition as you go.

Advanced Resources

- **Sed Cheat Sheet:** https://cheatography.com/heiko/cheat-sheets/sed/
- **Power Sed Book:** https://www.oreilly.com/library/view/sed-awk/1565922255/
- **Online Regex Testers:** https://regex101.com/ (Supports explaining regular expressions visually)

Sed is a deep tool. The more you use it for challenging tasks, the more tricks you'll discover!

Section 10:
Automating Tasks with Bash

Scripting for Automation: Basics

The ability to automate repetitive tasks is one of the most potent advantages of mastering Bash scripting. In this chapter, we'll introduce core automation concepts and build practical scripts to streamline your workflow.

The Power of Automation

Why should you invest time in automating tasks? Consider these benefits:

- **Reduced errors:** Scripts, once debugged, perform tasks consistently, minimizing human error.
- **Time savings:** Automating frequent chores frees up hours of your day.
- **Enhanced Scalability:** A script that works on a small dataset can often handle much larger tasks without modification.
- **Improved Workflows:** Automated steps become reliable building blocks within more complex workflows.

Identifying Tasks Ripe for Automation

Think about your daily computer work. Look for tasks that are:

- **Tedious:** Boring tasks become major motivation killers.

- **Time-consuming** Taking significant chunks of your workday.
- **Error-prone:** Tasks where you often have typos or forget necessary steps.
- **Repetitive across systems:** If you find yourself doing the same thing on multiple Linux/Unix/macOS machines.

Fundamental Automation Script Structure

While complexity will grow, most automation scripts share these elements:

1. **Shebang:** `#!/bin/bash` indicates your script uses the Bash interpreter.
2. **Comments:** Use '#" to explain what your script does and *why*, and comment complex code sections.
3. **Command sequences:** A series of commands you'd usually type at the command line, organized to do the task.
4. **Variables:** Can make your script dynamic, e.g., to adapt to filenames provided by the user.
5. **Error checking:** (More advanced, later) Incorporating logic to gracefully handle issues like missing files.

Example 1: File Cleanup

Let's automate deleting old log files:

```bash
#!/bin/bash

# Specify the directory to clean up
log_dir="/var/log/"

# Find log files older than 7 days and delete
find "$log_dir" -name "*.log" -mtime +7 -delete
```

Example 2: File Compression with User Input

```bash
#!/bin/bash

# Accept a filename from the user
read -p "Enter the filename to compress: "
filename

# Compress the file
gzip "$filename"

echo "$filename has been compressed!"
```

Automation Best Practices

- **Start small:** Begin with simple automation tasks. Success will breed motivation.
- **Test Thoroughly:** Especially when automating file deletions or system changes. Run scripts in a safe testing environment whenever possible.
- **Use version control (e.g., Git):** Allows you to safely experiment and revert to older versions of your scripts if needed.

Advanced Automation

In the next chapter, we'll cover techniques like:

- **Scheduling scripts:** Using 'cron' for routine, unattended execution.
- **Parameter handling:** Allowing scripts to be adaptable when run.
- **Sophisticated error handling:** Ensuring robust operation without manual intervention

Resources

- **The Linux 'find' command:** https://linux.die.net/man/1/find
- **Introduction to 'cron':** https://en.wikipedia.org/wiki/Cron
- **'The Bash Hackers Wiki' (Automation section):** http://wiki.bash-hackers.org/

Advanced Automation Techniques in Bash

In the previous chapter, you laid the foundation for automating tasks with Bash. Now, let's elevate your scripts with techniques used by professional developers and seasoned system administrators.

Handling Script Arguments

Allowing users to provide input makes your automation scripts far more flexible. Here's how:

- **1, 2, etc.:** These special variables hold command-line arguments passed to your script. For example, if you run `my_script.sh file1.txt backup.zip`, then 1 would be "file1.txt", and 2 would be "backup.zip".
- **$#:** This variable represents the total number of arguments passed.

Example: Flexible Image Conversion

```bash
#!/bin/bash

if [ $# -ne 2 ]; then
    echo "Usage: $0 <input_image> <output_format>"
    exit 1
fi

input_file=$1
output_format=$2
```

```
convert "$input_file"
"$input_file.$output_format"  # Using
ImageMagick's 'convert'
echo "Conversion complete!"
```

Scheduling with Cron

Cron is a powerful tool for unattended script execution at specific times.

- **Crontab:** Each user has a 'crontab' file defining schedules. Edit it with `crontab -e`.

Example: Daily Cleanup

Add this line to your crontab:

0 0 * * * /path/to/your/cleanup_script.sh

This runs your 'cleanup_script.sh' at midnight (0 0) every day (* * *).

Mastering Input and Output Redirection

- **> (Output redirection):** Send script output to a file instead of the screen. Ex: `my_script.sh > log.txt`
- **< (Input redirection):** Feed a file as input to a script. Ex: `sort < list.txt`
- **Pipes (|):** Chain commands, the output of one becomes the input to the next. Ex: `ls -l | grep "Aug"` lists files, piping the result to 'grep' to show only lines containing "Aug".

Example: Report Generation

```
#!/bin/bash
```

```
df -h > disk_report.txt  # Get disk usage
top -b -n 1 | head -n 10 >> disk_report.txt  #
Append top processes
```

Process Management with Backgrounding and Signals

- **& (Backgrounding):** Run a script in the background by adding '&' after the command. Ex: `my_long_task.sh &`
- **jobs:** Lists your background processes.
- **fg:** Brings a backgrounded task to the foreground.
- **kill %job_number:** Sends a termination signal to a background job.
- **Other signals:** Like 'kill -HUP' (hangup) to trigger some applications to re-read configuration.

Robust Error Handling

- **Conditional Execution:** Use '&&' (execute next command if the previous succeeded) and '||' (execute next command only if the previous failed)
- **Traps:** Intercept signals (Ctrl-C, etc.). Use the 'trap' command. This could involve graceful cleanup in your script before interruption.

Example: Enhanced Backup

```
#!/bin/bash

backup_dir="/backups/"
timestamp=$(date +%Y%m%d)

tar -czf "$backup_dir"website_$timestamp.tar.gz
/var/www/html || {
    echo "Backup failed!" | mail -s "Backup Error"
your_email@example.com
    exit 1
```

```
}

echo "Backup successful!"
```

Resources

- **Explaining Shell Arguments:**
  http://tldp.org/LDP/Bash-Beginners-Guide/html/sect_09_07.
  html
- **Crontab Guru:** https://crontab.guru/ (Helps create cron
  schedules)
- **Linux Signals:**
  https://man7.org/linux/man-pages/man7/signal.7.html

Section 11:
Bash Scripting for System Administration

Basic System Administration through Bash

As a system administrator, the ability to automate and streamline processes using Bash scripting is an invaluable skill. In this chapter, we'll explore foundational system management tasks and how to tackle them with the power of the command line and Bash scripts.

Understanding the System Administrator's Role

System administrators maintain the uptime, performance, and security of computers and networks. Bash scripting lets you:

- **Monitor system health:** Check vital statistics like disk space and CPU usage.
- **Manage users and groups:** Automate user creation and modifications.
- **Install and update software:** Write scripts to deploy packages easily.
- **Enforce security policies:** Implement checks and configurations.
- **Backup and restore data:** Simplify the process and add safeguards.

Checking System Health

Let's start with fundamental tools for getting system information:

- **uptime:** Get a quick view of system load and how long it's been running.
- **df:** View free space on drives and partitions.
- **free:** Monitor memory (RAM) usage.
- **top/htop:** Interactive views of running processes (htop is often friendlier).

Example: Disk Space Alert

```bash
#!/bin/bash

threshold=90  # Alert if a filesystem exceeds 90%
usage

df -h | awk '{print $5 " " $6}' | grep -v Use% |
while read usage mountpoint; do
    if [ $usage -ge $threshold ]; then
        echo "Warning: $mountpoint at ${usage}%!"
| mail -s "Disk Alert"
your_admin_email@domain.com
    fi
done
```

User Management Basics

- **useradd:** Create new user accounts.
- **usermod:** Modify existing user properties (password, groups, etc.).
- **userdel:** Delete user accounts.
- **passwd:** Set and change user passwords.
- **/etc/passwd:** File containing user account information.

Example: Password Expiry Check

```
#!/bin/bash
passwd_file="/etc/shadow"

cat "$passwd_file" | cut -d: -f1,5 | while read
user expiry_days; do
    if [ "$expiry_days" -gt 90 ]; then
        echo "$user password expiring soon,
please update!"
    fi
done
```

Package Management Automation

(Note: Package commands differ across distributions: apt/dpkg on Debian/Ubuntu, yum/dnf on RHEL-based, etc.)

- **apt update / yum update:** Update package lists.
- **apt install / yum install :** Install software.

Example: Security Updates

```
#!/bin/bash

if [[ $(id -u) -ne 0 ]]; then  # Check if running
as root
    echo "Run this script as root! "
    exit 1
 fi

apt update && apt upgrade -y  # For Debian/Ubuntu
systems
```

System Administration Best Practices

- **Documentation:** Comment your scripts to keep track of their purpose.
- **Permissions:** Be mindful of script permissions to ensure security.
- **Superuser (root) privileges:** Exercise caution! Scripts run as root have unrestricted system access.

Resources

- **Linux Commands Cheat Sheet:** https://www.linuxtrainingacademy.com/linux-commands-cheat-sheet/
- **Your Distribution's Package Manager Docs:** Look these up online specific to the Linux flavor you use.

Challenge: System Audit Script

Can you write a script that gathers the following and saves it to a report file?

- Installed packages
- Current logged-in users
- Running services

Conclusion & Additional Resources

Congratulations! If you've worked through the chapters of this book, you've gained a mastery of Bash scripting that sets you apart. You can now transform tedious tasks into automated workflows, confidently tackle system administration challenges, and solve unique problems with the power of the command line.

Reflecting on Your Scripting Journey

Take a moment to think about where you started:

- Do those 'magic' one-liners that used to baffle you now make sense?
- Are you itching to find new tasks to automate, to further flex your scripting muscles?
- Do you find yourself looking at everyday computer work through a new lens, considering how a script might simplify it?

If so, the goal of this book has been achieved!

The Path Goes Ever Onward

Bash scripting is a gateway to an even larger universe of tools and programming concepts:

- **More robust languages:** If your scripts become very complex, exploring Python or Perl offers better structure for large projects.

- **Web Scripting:** Dive into JavaScript (client-side) and languages like PHP or Node.js (server-side) to control websites and make them dynamic.
- **DevOps Methodology:** Automation is at the heart of DevOps. Bash skills lay the groundwork for configuration management tools like Ansible or Terraform.

Resources to Continue Learning

The online world offers a wealth of resources to support your ongoing Bash escapades:

- **The Linux Documentation Project:** Packed with in-depth guides and manuals https://tldp.org/
- **Stack Overflow - Bash Tag:** Find solutions to specific problems or help troubleshoot https://stackoverflow.com/questions/tagged/bash
- **Reddit - r/bash and r/linuxadmin:** Communities for exchanging tips and discussion https://www.reddit.com/r/bash/ https://www.reddit.com/r/linuxadmin/
- **Online Courses:** Platforms like Udemy or Coursera often have Bash-focused or general scripting courses

Sharing Your Creations

- **Document your scripts:** Make future-you grateful, even small comments save the day!
- **Script Repositories:** Once you have polished projects, consider sharing them on sites like GitHub. This connects you with a larger community, helps others, and you might get great feedback to advance your own skills.

Advice for Mastering Any Skill

Bash, like many technical skills, is best learned through practice.

- **Set goals:** "Learn Bash" is vague. Instead, pick projects: "Write a script to organize my music library," etc.
- **Learn from others:** Look at how other people create scripts. Borrow good ideas shamelessly!
- **Never stop testing:** Bash lets you do powerful things, which also means potential for mishaps. Always test your scripts thoroughly.

Final Thoughts

The art of command-line scripting isn't just about efficiency; it's about understanding your computing environment at a deeper level and bending it to your will. Embrace the creativity that Bash scripting encourages, and let it unlock the true potential of working with Linux, Unix, and macOS systems.

Thank you for reading! Now go forth and script amazing things!

www.ingramcontent.com/pod-product-compliance
Lightning Source LLC
Chambersburg PA
CBHW080537060326
40690CB00022B/5162